I want to say **thank you** t
To know that my words c
single person is the most amazing gift I
could've ever thought of receiving. Never in
my life would I have thought I would publish
any of my poems, they were always this
secret I kept for only my journal to see. And
here I am, literally an open book showing
you all the deep insides of my mind, the
inside of my actual journals. Because that's
the support you all have showed me, support
that feels like friendship, support that feels
like trust.

And I am *forever* thankful for that.

With so much love,

Emma Rose Harris

Find me awake in your dreams,
He told her,
Just as you fall asleep,
I'll start to wake up,
We can move across universes,
Holding those same hands,
That I've always known,
We can watch the stars,
From your dream eyes,
Or we can step in the sweet memories,
I've forgotten at once,
Time is endless in a dream,
A soft,
Velvet dream,
Time will never slip from our fingertips,
Like it did in the past,
The only place where time is on your side,
A soft,
Velvet Dream

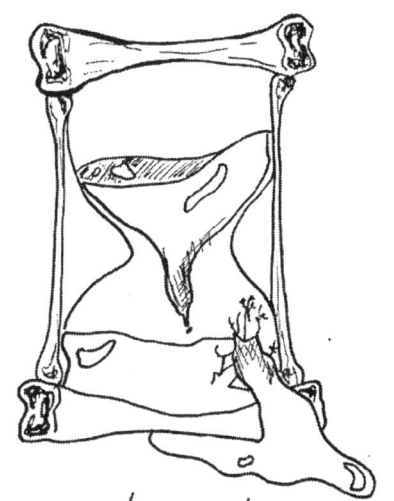

I keep longing to wake up,
In a different time,
Its like I can't keep growing older,
Without you by my side.

Forget I ever existed,
In this world that we lived in,
Together just us,
No god up above,
This heaven we were in,
Just turned into hell,
Now everywhere I go,
I'm reminded of you,
The pictures, the smells,
I know them all too well

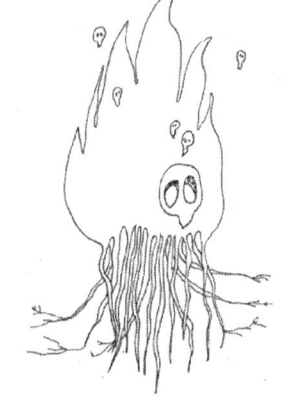

Some days I'm so focused on nothing,
I can't seem to help you or myself,
I think and I think,
But I can't even remember what my thoughts were about,
I get lost in time,
And I drift into the void,
A soft oblivion,
Even to me, unknown.
Sometimes I'm just a blank face,
I can't remember half the things you said,
I can't even remember what I said in return,
And some days,
I can't seem to remember why everything hurts.

Melt me down till im nothing but bones,
Sing my name till you run out of songs,
Make me feel like im not all alone,
Use my brain till its turned into stone,
Touch my body that you believe you own,
Make me your muse til you run out of booze,
And when you sober up and forget all my love,
I just want you to remember,
I always believed you were getting better

The flowers you gave me,
Just died like you said,
And I let them dry up,
And hang on my wall instead,
The red ones got dark,
Hardened but fragile,
And the white ones,
Turned dim, brown, and feathered,
They hung there for a year,
With all your old cards and letters,
Couple months before you died,
I lit those flowers on fire,
I promise myself I wouldnt remember,
The pain you had caused me,
That cold December,

Oh, the pain I thought would last
    forever,
If only I'd have known,
<u>That</u> pain was so much better,

The light seeps in the cracks of the forest,
My dreams seep into reality,
My love for you is nothing short of insanity,
My human wishes are still the vanity,
I dream of you touching me,
Like the sun stretches its arms,
So far out,
Just to reach and touch the trees,
I dream that you can reach me,
I dream your arms spread as far,
As these sunny rays caressing me,
I dream your lips are just a touch,
Just a touch away from me,

At night when I am dying,
Next to you is where I'm lying,
Lie to me,
And tell me,
I look fine,
My eyes have dried out,
There's nothing left to cry,
These blood shot lines,
Toxifying whats inside,
You told me stay the same,
But somehow I have changed,
And everytime I lie,
You take it by suprise,
I can no longer cry,

I can no longer cry,
The darkest of my days,
You took the pain away,
And somehow, I forgot,
To thank you along the way,
I wish we'd just go back,
Back when we were kids,
When everything that happened,
Was just the way it is,
No future,
No tomorrow,
No hearts left just to borrow,
To twist and break and hollow,
To end up being swallowed

Without you I'd be dead,
So I'll drain your body,
From whats inside,
And drink your blood,
To save my life,
At night when I am dying,
Next to you is where I'm lying,
Your ashes piled next to mine

Your empty sometimes
Not just empty of words,
Empty inside,
Your heart seems drained,
Draining as we speak,
The blood that runs through you,
Has you weak to your own knees,
You cant love someone, w
With a heart so un-full,
You cant love someone,
Who doesnt love you

I cried my own eyes dry,
I peeled my own flesh clean,
And to think back on it,
I dont even know what any of it means,
I try so hard to understand people,
I end up torturing myself,
Diving into the minds of other people,
Avoiding my own self,
Making up screenplays,
So, I dont have to face my reality,
Pretending I know what you mean,
As I listen from a distance,
Off in my dreams,
Off in real life,
Im as off as it seems

Ive lost the words I want to say to you,
Its like theyve all been forgotten,
I cant seem to put my emotions into words,
Theyve seem to all gone rotten,
Not only have I lost myself,
But memories seem to have subsided.

Even with a twisted spine,
She carried on,
Bruised,
Broken,
Shattered

Death has a way with me,
It always has,
I feel it following me,
Everywhere I go,
Its soft footprints linger,
As I move around the globe,
Touching the one I love,
Like hes got some kind of control,
Maybe Im what he wants,
But he just cant find the hold,
Id rather it be me taken,
Then anyone else left I know

It seems harder to remember the good,
The bad just has a way of sticking,
I guess those times alone,
Crying in your room,
Really did end up forever hurting,
And those times everyone said,
Would only get better,
Were the only ones that ever left scarring,

How nice it would be if the beginning-
Ever felt as strong as the departing

I'm stuck in the past,
Thinking nothing will last,
And every time it does,
I wander off to look for more,
Nothing seems to satisfy me,
And when it does,
I run,
I run because I dont feel worthy enough,
Worthy enough of something so pure,
Untainted, clear and light,
But the light is burning, my love,
Like stepping outside,
In the bright sun for the first time in days,
I cant seem to open my eyes,
All I want is the shade,
Your light is so blinding,
I seem to want it to fade,
Untainted clear and light,
I cant choose my wrongs from right

The soul I needed,
Was slowly depleting,
Into the thin, thin air,
Like droplets of dew,
That sat on my roof,
From all the rain that never fell,
The air I breathed in,
As you whispered to tell me,
That the world that we live in,
Would soon too fall as well,
The whispers they echoed,
In the caves of my ears,
The words would get trapped,
Just for me only to hear,
The world that we live in,
Would soon too fall as well,
I wish I knew,
What to do,
The moment you told me,
We were all so doomed,
I wish I knew how to say goodbye,
Before the world started to burn,
Right before my dewy eyes

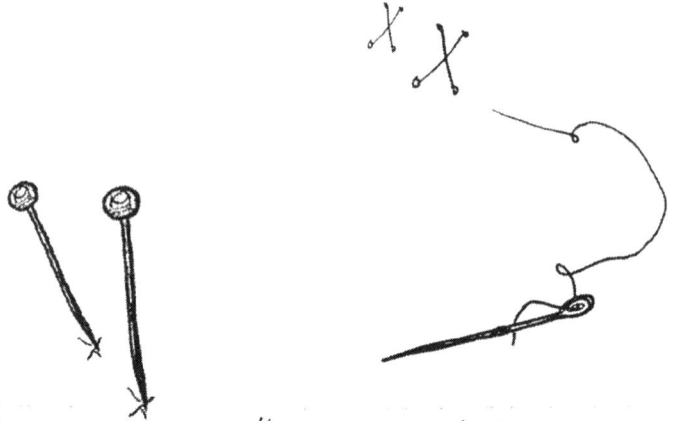

Letting the worst things come between us,
I'm becoming everything I swear I wouldn't,
Everything you swear you wanted,
Is everything I'm getting rid of,
You want me for someone I'm not anymore,
I want you for someone you never were

Every night my mind raced as fast as it could,
And in my dreams,
I always tried to catch up with you

I keep thinking we were supposed to be together,
Every fucking time I close my eyes,
I think of the times id lay with you right beside me, And I cant help but to regret all the times I didn't tell you how much I need you, Now everytime I close my eyes,
I think of you, and thats all I have left.
I'll never see you again, and it hurts to know all I have left is just in my head.
Sometimes I make myself believe,
You are still right here next to me,
But in the middle of the night,
I try to open my eyes,
To the world that you how live in,
I ask to see you,
But it never seems to come true,
I just wish there was someone left to talk to

I had a dream you didn't love me anymore,
You were too used to hearing it,
And although your gone,
It still hurt more than ever,
To hear the word, I solemnly remember,
The word love off your lips,
With hopeless meaning,
And a sad, sad twist,
And to tell you the truth,
Somedays I struggle with the thought,
The thought that you never loved me,
I dont have you left to ask,
I dont have you to reassure me.

Lately I feel too loud,
Like I'm screaming,
But no one understands what I'm saying,
Like the whole world is watching me,
Open my mouth so wide,
As they tell my stories for me,
But there just watching me,
Thats all they seem to do,
They cant hear me,
They dont understand,
Is there anyone around,
Who understands what its like,
To be so loud no one can hear you

I know what its like,
When your nights full of cries,
Oh my god,
Why is this happening to me,
I knew itd happen to me,
Is it my fault,
My negative thoughts,
Is it my fault,
I always thought something like this would,
Is that why it did,
Youve been lying in the dirt,
For years now,
Is it all my fault

Afraid to share these feelings,
They might be all I have,
Look into my eyes,
You might mistake that I'm alive,
All whats left,
Are these emotions,
That are eating at my head,
My brain is now my food,
I'm eating myself alive,
And everytime I think of you,
I think that I might die.
My heart skips two beats,
Lying on my side,
Someone told me these pills,
Would help with the pain,
So here I am again,
Sickening my brain

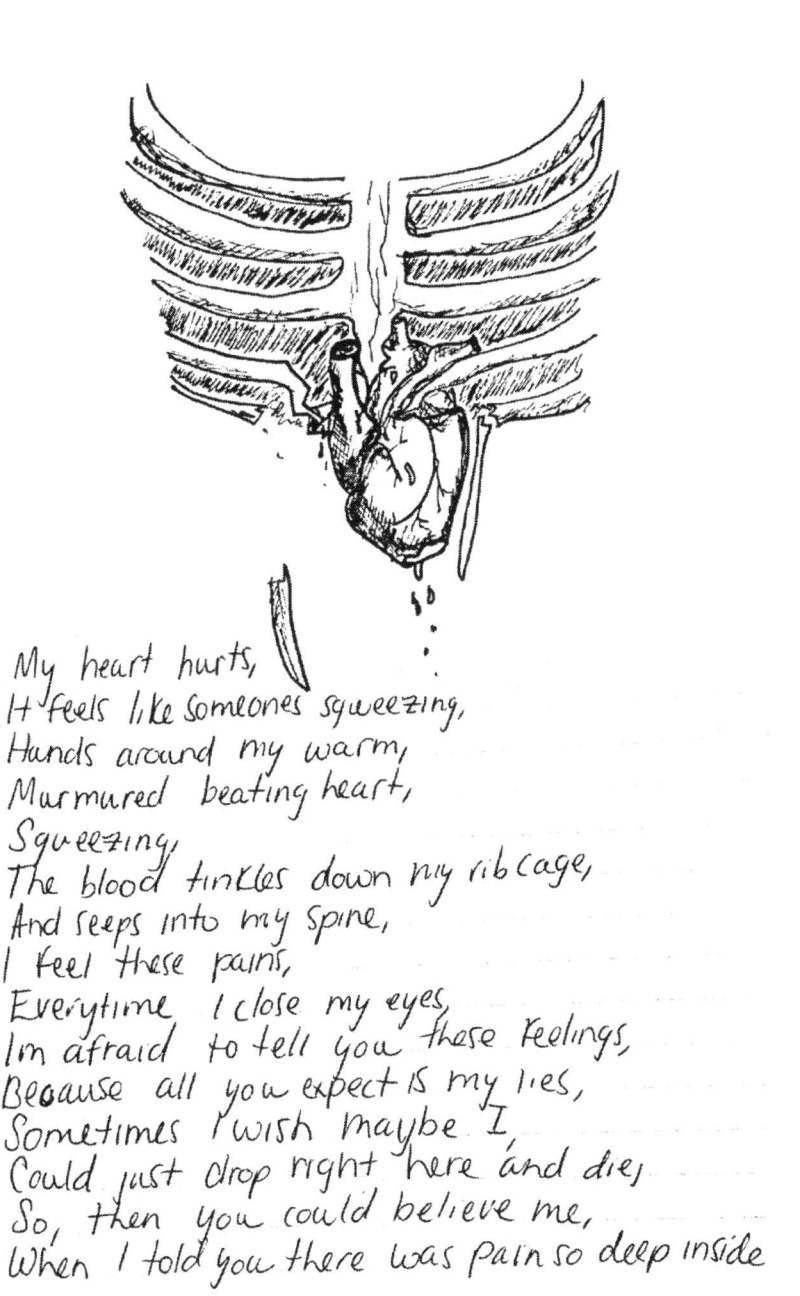

My heart hurts,
It feels like someones squeezing,
Hands around my warm,
Murmured beating heart,
Squeezing,
The blood tinkles down my rib cage,
And seeps into my spine,
I feel these pains,
Everytime I close my eyes,
I'm afraid to tell you these feelings,
Because all you expect is my lies,
Sometimes I wish maybe I,
Could just drop right here and die,
So, then you could believe me,
When I told you there was pain so deep inside

I understand you,
When you don't believe me,
Well at least I can say I try,
I tried so many times,
To explain how I felt...
And I lied,
It just comes so natural,
Falls right off the tongue.
The person you seem to want,
Is the person I've outgrown

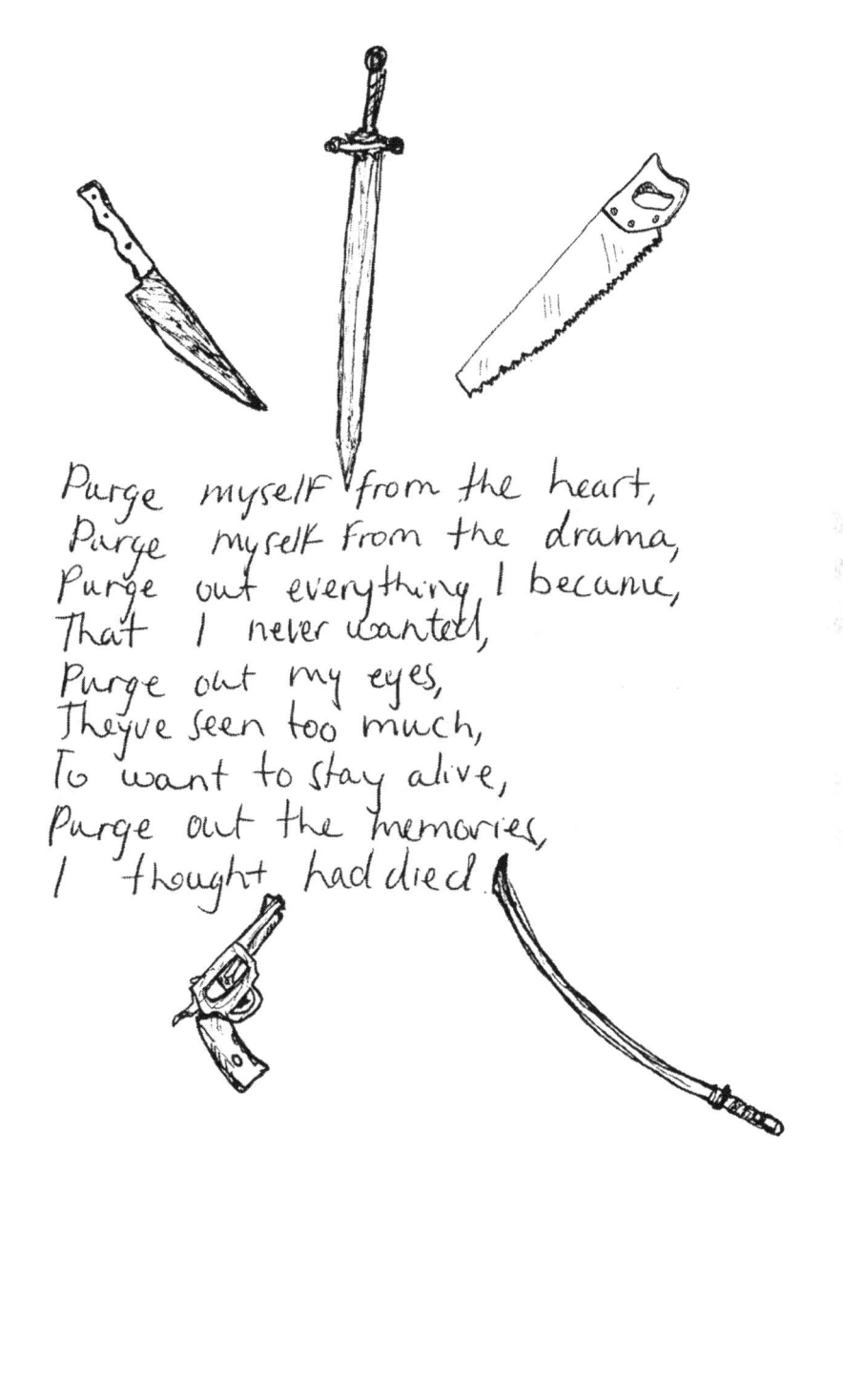

Purge myself from the heart,
Purge myself from the drama,
Purge out everything I became,
That I never wanted,
Purge out my eyes,
They've seen too much,
To want to stay alive,
Purge out the memories,
I thought had died.

It feels like I'm waking up underwater,
Every time I go to take a breath,
More water fills my lungs,
Holding on for dear life,
To nothing but a dream,
Willing to drown,
Just to hear your voices sweet sounds,
Waking up is a nightmare,
Even when I dream about you dying,
I still get to see that face,
Willing to drown,
Just to hear you call my name,
Even when I dream about you dying,
I still get to see your face

I steer you away from me,
Just to let you right back in,
Because everytime you leave me be,
I end up facedown,
Mouth full of the street,
This worlds too heavy without your hands,
Holding me

~~THIS ONES FUCKED~~

Is this the end,
I cant hear your words anymore,
All I can hear are the things I dont like,
I cant smile at you anymore,
All it leads to is a fight,
I crave a love that just doesnt exist,
I crave something,
And then I resist,
I want to give you one more chance,
I cant take this anymore,
The first time was enough,
Our fighting hurts my head,
Maybe I'd love you more if you were dead,
Just like I did him,
Why cant I write a poem,
Without dragging him in...

So will I really be yours forever,
For some reason its starting to feel temporary,
Which is scary because it never has,
Felt anything less than extraordinary,
How can something so beautiful,
Turn so ugly

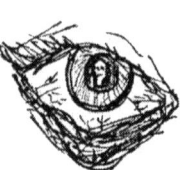

Do you know how it feels to think everyone you love is going to die? Like this may just be the last time you get to look into their eyes. Its a thought I want out, but it always seems to creep back in.

And I'm afraid I think it so much, I might give it the power to win.

I told you I loved you before I could explain,
The fucked up details inside of my brain,
But me and you seem to be the same,
But that was the same thing I told him,
Now I've pushed you away,
Further than ever,
Because my destructive ways have gotten the better,
I'll try and try to make you need me,
And right when you start to,
I'll leave you beneath me

My headlight shine right into your eyes,
Leap in front of me,
Suck out my mind,
Spit it back up with your corrupted thoughts,
I wanted you here and now I want you turned off,
The worlds a mess
You only make it worse,
This worlds a mess,
I cant find a home,
This worlds a mess,
I have no where to go,
My face still swollen from the liquid that poured out,
Look behind my rear view,
Start to hallucinate silhouettes of you
I see you in the dark,
I see you in my art,
Im sick of this one dimension life,
I need to feel at least the day and night,
I need to feel the other side,
Im sick of the way you play with my head,
Im sick of these thoughts decaying away,
My once pretty, perfect brain,
Has now become a damaged, old, tagged up grave,
Spider webbed and chained
Tell me you love me just the same,
Tell me you still love me,
The way that they say

The Flames seem ever so endearing,
I want to wrap myself in the warmth,
Maybe you could hold me close,
Closer than him at least,
I feel neglected,
Frozen in the snow,
I'm alone,
He's asleep,
I can never sleep,
Awake with the stars,
Just where I want to be,
Are you here?
Laying here with me,
Am I crazy?

If I'm hallucinating,
Just let me

You left me somewhere in the middle,
The middle of yesterday and today,
I am no longer the top of your thoughts,
I have sunken to the bottom,
I feel like a balloon thats about to pop,
Your foot smooshing me down,
Supressing my every atom,
Everytime I see you,
I miss you when youre gone,
And when your back...
I still miss you,
I also miss myself,
I havent seen her in about two years,
Maybe I am someone else by now,
But I miss who I was before,
I'll always miss who I was before,
Maybe I'll never get her back,
But I still look for her in you,
And when she doesnt show,
I end up missing him too...

She told me your here,
That your stuck here,
Stuck in the in between,
And the only reason why,
Is that your attatched to my side,
And the only way you can leave,
Is with some help from me,
But those words seemed so sweet,
Your attatched to me,
Ive decided,
I cannot "help you leave"

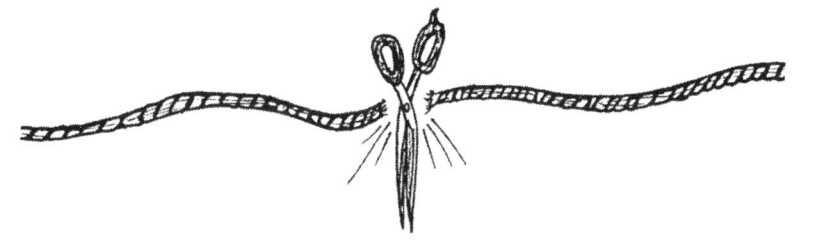

You were here,
You were there,
You were everywhere,
But when I really needed you,
All there was left,
Cold stares,
I thought it was love,
But in the end it was rough,
All you heard were my words,
Turned into meaningless blurbs
Words you didn't care to understand,
You didn't care to get deeper,
You didn't care to see clearer,
And I had to leave you in the muddy waters,
You let yourself soak in,
I can't be the one to guide you through,
All this glue you've piled yourself in

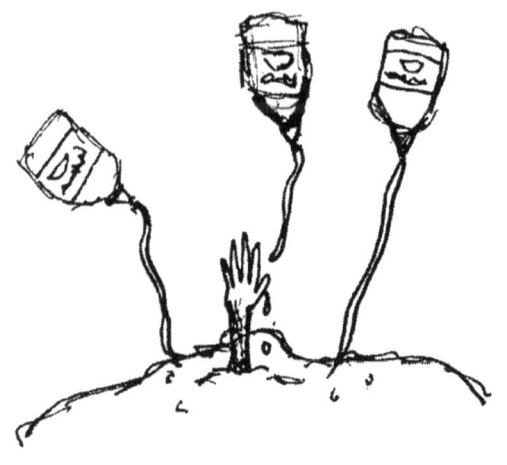

I dont think were much good for eachother,
Everyday I'm getting under your skin,
I tried to cut threw mine last night,
The blade was too dull,
Didnt quite reach my insides,
Havent done that in a while,
I cant figure out why,
Maybe it was to make you feel guilty,
Maybe the pain seemed better to bear,
Than these thoughts,
Thoughts of you leaving,
Why do I feel so stuck,
You tell him I speak of him too much,
Believe me, I know,
Im just having a really hard time trying to let go,
I try to for you,
To make you a little more happy,
But it seems like everything I do,
Your still stuck in your misery,
I dont think were much good for eachother,
Not anymore,
I told you to stay one last time,
~~But you escaped through your door~~

But you escaped through the door

Star crossed lovers,
with a terrible fate

I can't find the words to rhyme,
And maybe they don't have to,
Sometimes my brain feels like,
Someone sucked out all the juice,
And my heart feels like its dangling,
By one single vein out of chest,
Rib cage beaten and broken,
Chest caving in,
Sometimes it feels like you were my only friend
Sometimes I feel living without you,
Is a life I want to end

I feel nothing but half empty since you left,
I dont know how i'll ever feel full,
Theres a piece of me,
That was ripped away when you were too,
No matter how much water I put,
My glass still isnt half full

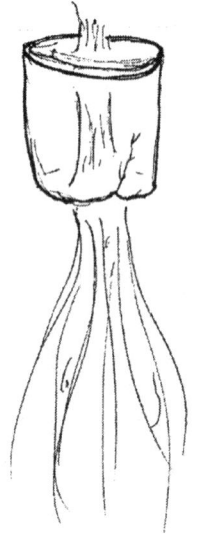

I had a dream you were here still;
I do this every so often. I told you,
you look different, healthier. You
told me you changed. You still
told me you loved me; In a voice
I've been starting to forget. But
the worst part about it,
when I wake up,
It all comes to an end.

Grief
I feel like its following me around,
I feel its eyes on me at all times,
And when I dare not to think about it,
It reminds me who Im messing with,
But I didnt sign up for this
And if I did, I forgot to read the waiver,
I want out of this
I want out forever,
I feel myself causing danger,
Im hiding under the covers,
But it likes to make itself comfortable,
Everytime I think Im free,
Its at my feet right below me,
Theres this pain in my brain,
And its driving me insane,
And everytime I let it go,
It welcomes itself back home,
I feel like its following me around,
I feel its eyes on me at all times,
And when I dare not to think of it,
It reminds me who Im messing with

Pastels in the sky,
The life in your eyes,
The voices in my head,
I know one day I'll be okay,
But what happens until then?
I'll sit here in silence,
Waiting for my world to end

You surround me in warmth,
but I still feel so cold

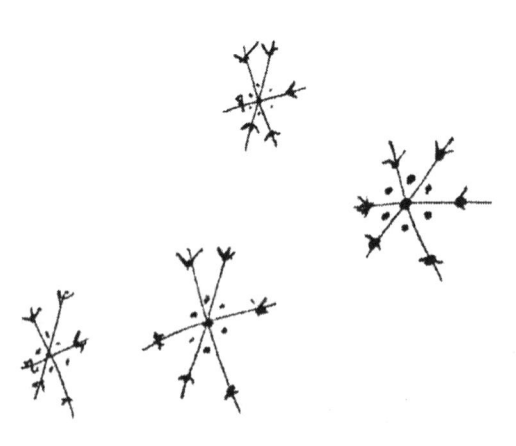

Dark but soft,
The inside of you warmed my heart,
But it also so easily tore me apart,
You take and you give,
And you take once more,
To distinguish what's mine now,
I'm not really quite sure

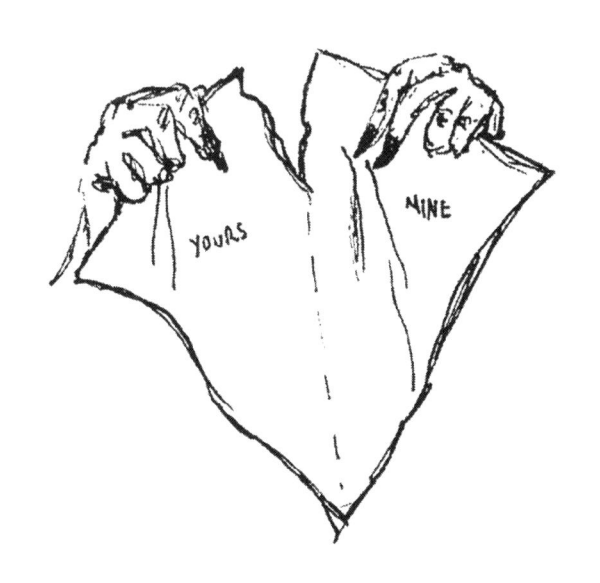

Do you ever feel afraid that one day.
you wont feel this anymore,
that one day our last breath to
each other will be a goodbye,
I cant seem to feel anything
for much too long,
I have this reoccuring dream
of an ocean I'm not the slightest
bit afraid of, I ride the biggest
waves and swim as deep down
as I can without worrying about
my breath...
I wish that was how love is,
but I'm so afraid of that last breath

Baby you're like a broken clock
I keep trying to fix,
And each time I manage to get
a piece out,
The new one just doesn't fit

I had a dream I could bring you back to life,
I have many dreams like this,
Some days it feels like my dreams
Are just an alternate reality,
A reality where you're still here,
Where life and death doest have the power
to tear us apart,
Some days I long to be asleep in that
      dream,
  forever

...Somedays pretending to be okay is the only way to survive

8 Somedays living in a dream, is the only way to still feel alive

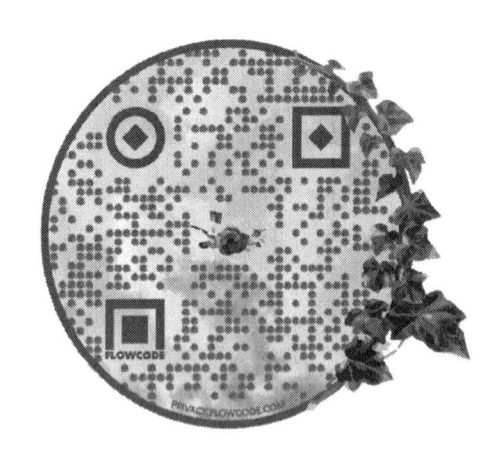

TO FIND MORE FROM THIS
AUTHOR, SIMPLY SCAN
THIS CODE USING YOUR
CELLPHONE CAMERA.

Printed in Great Britain
by Amazon